I0101101

Easy Book Promotion

A Step-by-Step Guide to Being Discovered

Cynthia Readnower

Easy Book Promotion
A Step-by-Step Guide to Being Discovered

Cynthia Readnower

Published by Skinny Leopard Media, Sarasota, FL

ISBN: 978-0-9899893-6-7

Table of Contents

Introduction

There are many people that will tell you that you need to "launch" your book and do all sorts of things to make sure your book hits the market and makes a big splash. Some authors try to make all their friends buy the book on the same day so that they can achieve an Amazon "bestseller" status. But truly, if you only get that bestseller badge for one day, within two weeks, Amazon will take it away from you because you haven't sustained the sales. Real marketing of your book requires *continual effort* and doesn't just involve a big launch or hitting the bestseller status for one day. If that's what you want, it just may be your ego, instead of your business smarts, that wants it.

Years ago, I heard a publisher speak and he said the only reason to write a book was if you just couldn't stand *not* to. You had to have a book inside of you just bursting to get out, then find an agent and a publisher. But with the advent of independent publishing and Amazon, it's easier than ever before. New tools that help you write, edit, publish and promote are always being developed. Now, there truly is no reason *not* to write a book if you want to. That being said, the competition now is fiercer than ever before, and Amazon, with 80% of the eBook market, has millions of books for sale, as well as having millions of print versions too.

So how do you stand out from the rest of the pack? The realty of the book market is that most books will sell a few copies and not make the authors much money. However, you can be smarter about it, make an effort to get visibility and do things to get more exposure. That's what this workbook is about. It will walk you through several different techniques to get more exposure, help you promote your book and hopefully get you more sales, without spending a ton of money.

I've tried to make these techniques as easy to use as possible but if you have trouble, I am a big fan of researching online and looking at the tutorials of others who have already conquered these approaches. No one knows your book better than you, no one has put as much time and effort in creating it and designing it as you. Use all that passion to promote it, put yourself out there and don't be afraid of trying something new. There may be a learning curve to some of the techniques but it is not insurmountable, just take it step by step. I'm enthusiastic for using what works and eliminating the rest so if you find a technique that brings in the fans, stick with it.

Chapter One
First Things First

If you've already written your book, skip ahead. If not, you need to figure out just where the idea you have fits into the book market. Search online for the topic you want to write and look at your competition. Even if there are already books like the one you have planned out there, it doesn't mean you can't offer a fresh perspective or come up with a new idea or unique approach. But it does mean, you are being savvy to do the research first and make the best possible choice for *your* book. The research may enable you to figure out a plot twist or a special way for you to stand out from the rest, especially if it is nonfiction.

Your book is your "baby." It truly is a process of giving birth to an idea, a creation that often comes from the heart. You have to be proud of it; you have to make sure that it reflects you in all your radiance, your knowledge, your talent and your creativity. You also deserve to have the tools to market it, after you've put so much time into creating it.

Are you writing fiction?

Fiction sells more than nonfiction. Overall, the top categories are Romance, Mysteries, and Science Fiction. But there are numerous sub-categories and if you can write your book in such a way to fit perfectly into one of those, you stand a better chance of competing than just in a huge general category. So if you want a greater chance at someone finding your book, target it to a smaller niche. For example: Romance->Historical Romance->Scottish *OR* Literature & Fiction -> United States -> African American -> Urban *OR* Science Fiction & Fantasy -> Fantasy -> Fairy Tales. You can see how the category gets narrowed down to something quite specific. Of course you may not be prepared to write a book on that narrow of a subject, but you get the gist. Drill down your category list till you find a niche you can compete in, if possible.

The best way to do this is to search the bestsellers that may be similar to your book idea on Amazon and then look down the page at the categories the book is in and what their rank is. You will find these categories toward the bottom of the book's page, usually right above the information about the author.

Product details

File Size: 5958 KB
Print Length: 156 pages
Publisher: Skinny Leopard Media (May 18, 2015)
Publication Date: May 18, 2015
Sold by: Amazon Digital Services LLC
Language: English
ASIN: B00XWTWX56
Text-to-Speech: Enabled
X-Ray: Not Enabled
Word Wise: Enabled
Lending: Enabled
Screen Reader: Supported
Enhanced Typesetting: Enabled
Amazon Best Sellers Rank: #980,389 Paid in Kindle Store (See Top 100 Paid in Kindle Store)
   #59 in Kindle Store > Kindle eBooks > Business & Money > Entrepreneurship & Small Business > **Franchises**
   #135 in Books > Business & Money > Small Business & Entrepreneurship > **Franchises**
   #999 in Kindle Store > Kindle eBooks > Business & Money > Entrepreneurship & Small Business > Entrepreneurship > **Startups**

Are you writing nonfiction?

What do you have to use as credibility? Most nonfiction requires a credible source (that's you). Do you have special education or training in the subject? Do you have advanced degrees? Do you have some type of experience with the subject that you can use as being unique? Did something happen to you that doesn't usually happen to other people? Have you achieved something very difficult to do? Does the subject elicit emotions in other people (dogs, children, cute pictures, etc.)? Have you figured out a system to save people time? Can you solve a problem? Can you enhance people's lives? Can you give someone an emotional or mental boost? Can you help people cope? Have you been to places that others are interested in? Can you coach them in a sport? Have you found a way to help someone learn a new language in an easier manner?

There is no end to the possible subject matter here, however, you are not only competing with other books, you are also competing with all the free information on the Internet, how-to videos, and social media that reflects hundreds of free trial offers. I urge you to research the category you want to write first to see what is already out there. If you want to write a diet book, you need to know what is selling and how you can make your pitch so that it is something different than anyone has seen before.

My book idea:

_____

_____

_____

_____

_____

Top books that are my competition:

_____

_____

_____

_____

_____

Who are the well-known authors in this market?

_____

_____

_____

_____

_____

How my book is unique from the others:

_____

_____

_____

_____

_____

_____

_____

_____

_____

_____

What book categories would it fit into?

_____

_____

_____

_____

_____

Chapter Two
Writing the Darn Book

If you're lucky, you will just sit still, tune in and the book will pour through your fingers into the keyboard. If you're like most people, it may happen once in a while, but the rest of the time will require discipline, continued effort and the ability to stay with it. Because most of us are doing this on the side, we still have other responsibilities such as a job, family, housework, car maintenance, and everything else that involves day-to-day living. Setting aside time to continue and complete your work usually requires discipline.

You can learn, though, a few methods to keep the words coming. I started writing a newspaper column fifteen years ago and I used to sit at the keyboard and try to come up with an idea. Sometimes it was grueling, but sometimes not. In the good times, I would almost hear the words in my head before they came out of my fingers, but the tough times could make me very frustrated and I would have to walk away. Over the years, I learned to relax and do some word/topic associations to start the flow. I often looked at my book shelves, pulled out some books and tried to see if any of the topics made sense to me and if there was some sort of *new way* of putting several ideas or topics together to come up with a column. After many years, I often just take a shower, or meditate and see if an idea pops in and then it does seem to pour out much more easily.

For example, try the book bubble chart. Start with a main topic in the center and then put all sorts of descriptive words in the smaller bubbles, or sub-topics, or scenes or whatever feels right.

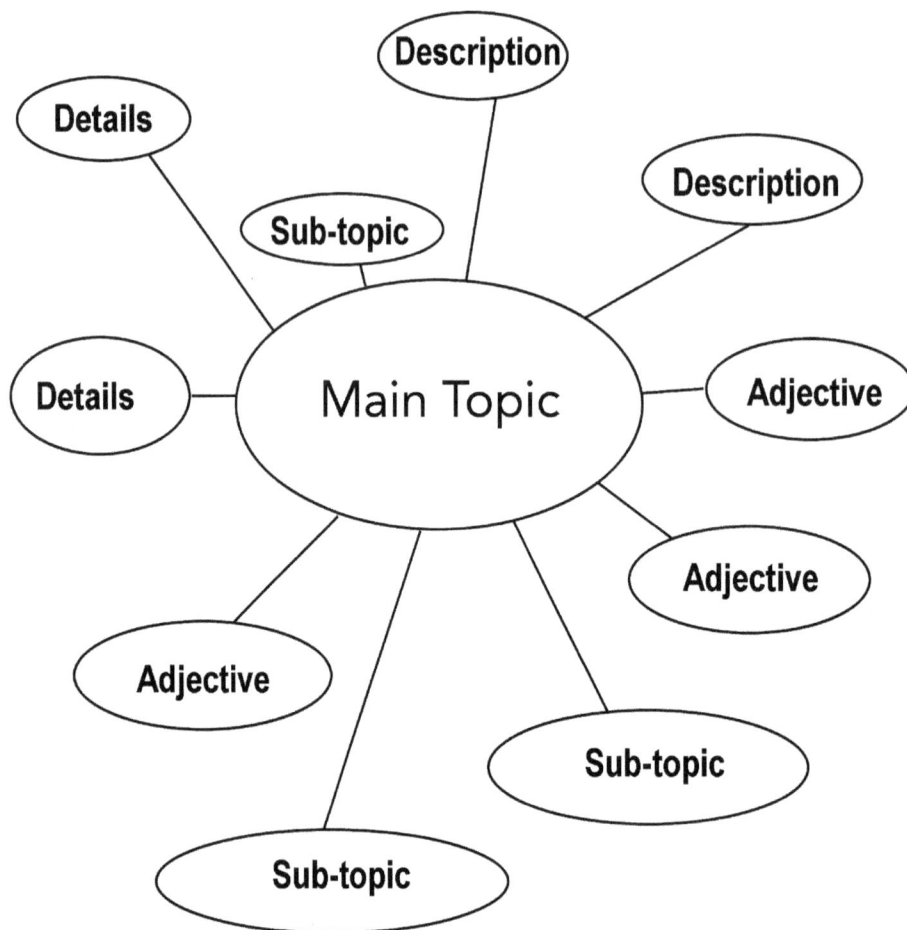

My example: I started with the topic "Dog Training" and filled in the bubbles with my ideas or musings. Then looking at the chart, I might decide to write about "Using Technology to Train Your Dog" or "How to Train an Adopted Dog Who May Have Been Abused." Those ideas stood out to me, what about you?

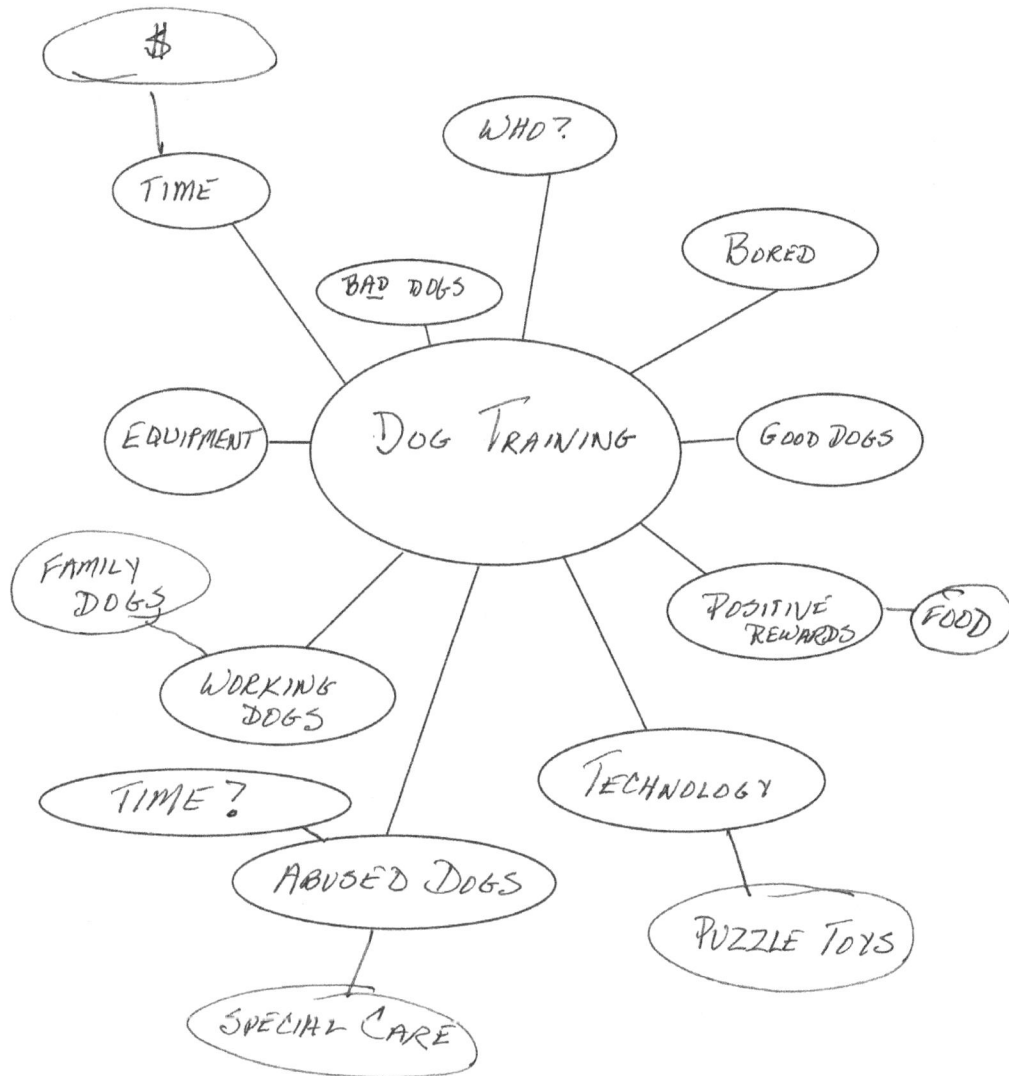

$ → TIME

WHO?

BAD DOGS

BORED

EQUIPMENT

DOG TRAINING

GOOD DOGS

FAMILY DOGS

WORKING DOGS

POSITIVE REWARDS → FOOD

TIME?

ABUSED DOGS

TECHNOLOGY

PUZZLE TOYS

SPECIAL CARE

Here are some sheets to get you started:

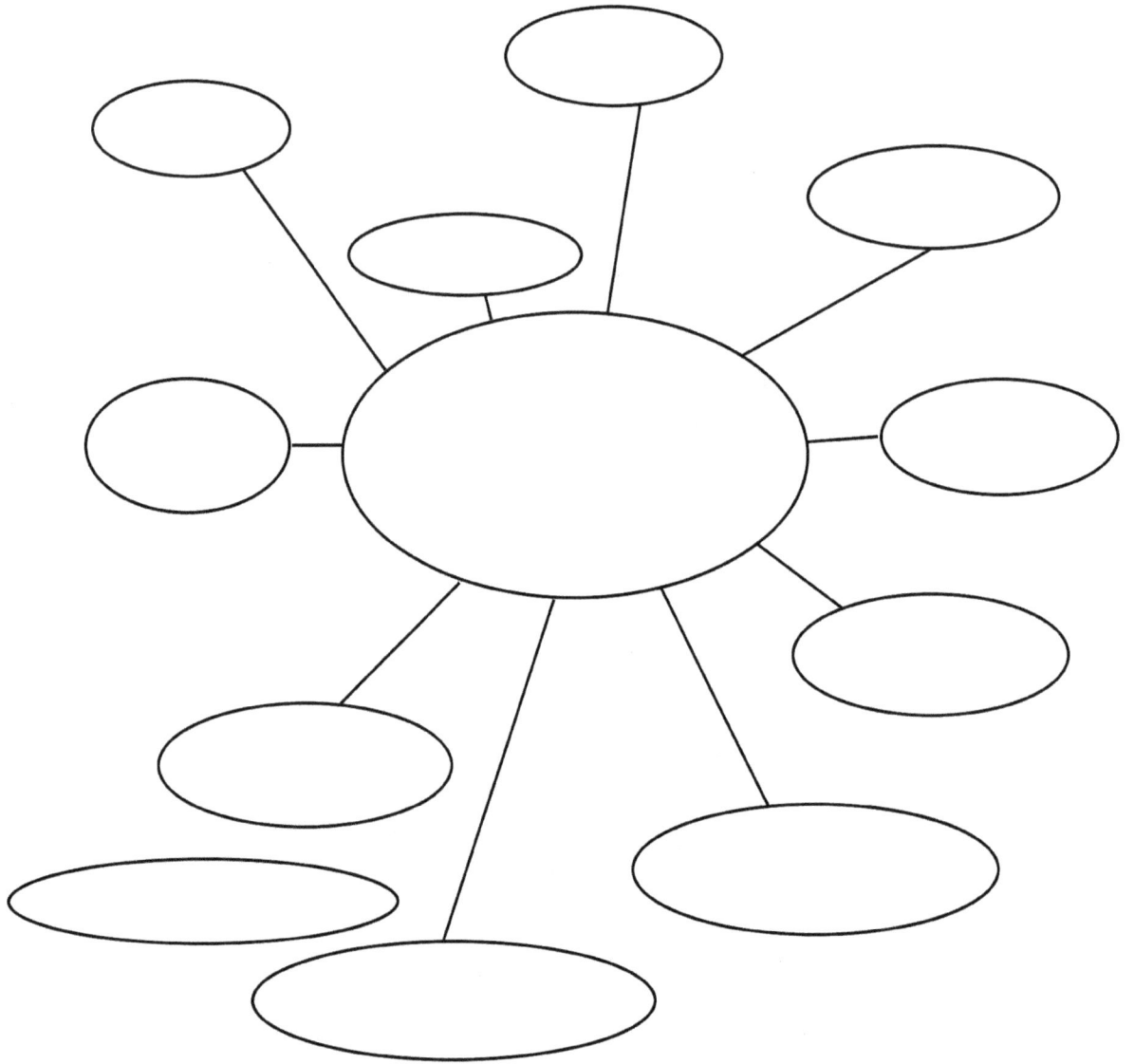

Your writing checklist: What you need to know to publish your book.

1. After you have written your book and perhaps re-written your book, you should edit it for grammar, spelling and proper phrasing. You can hire an editor, use editing software or have several friends proofread it. But it should be as perfect as you can make it. People are brutal on reviews when it comes to improper grammar and spelling.

2. Decide if you want it in both an eBook format and Print version. If you don't want to learn how to do this, then hire an Indie publisher. You should also consider an audio book, to cover all bases. Audio books require very stringent recording specifications and some really good audio equipment (not necessarily expensive).

   See Amazon's ACX audible book requirements here:
   https://audible-acx.custhelp.com/app/answers/detail/a_id/6736/~/what-are-the-acx-audio-submission-requirements%3F)

3. What size printed book do you want? I recommend that you decide this even before you start typing, if possible. It will give you an idea of how the words will look on the page size. If you want to see what IngramSpark's standard book sizes are (IngramSpark is a division of Ingram, the largest book distributor in the world. It is their author publishing division), go to:
   https://www.ingramspark.com/plan-your-book/print/book-types
   Click on the button near the bottom right that says, "trim sizes."

4. Who will design your book cover? Remember that a busy cover is not always best. A cover should give a reader an immediate sense of what type of book it is and it should be able to stand out amongst hundreds of other thumbnails.

5. Do you have images for your book? If so, the print version needs to be 300 DPI resolution for good print quality. Color will cost almost twice as much as only black and white to print, but there is no charge for using color on an eBook. Even if you have just

one color image in an entire print book, the whole cost is increased because of the paper required.

6. Create an author bio. What makes you different? Have you had unusual life experiences?

7. Create a book summary. Think of how to intrigue a reader to read your book. Read lots of summaries across other book platforms to get a feel for what catches your attention.

8. Write a dedication, if desired. Dedications usually thank someone for their support.

9. Get an ISBN number for the print version if the publisher does not supply one. (MyIdentifiers.com). Amazon will supply their own identification number for an eBook.

10. Get a Library of Congress number (LCCN) for the print version from the publisher. This is not absolutely necessary but the more that libraries start to inventory Indie published books, it will be required in the future. This is how a library catalogs books.

11. Create a disclaimer for your book, especially if you are giving advice. There are many samples online that can be used to create one. Disclaimers help to alleviate liability in the case someone uses your advice and doesn't like the results, but of course it is not foolproof.

12. Make sure the format of your book (margins, headers and footers, spacing, etc.) adheres to the size that you want the final printed book to be.

13. If you plan to file a copyright (you should), open an account at copyright.gov. If you file electronically, it is only $35. You will upload a file of your book digitally.

14. If you are selling a book on Amazon, after it is published you can go to AuthorCentral.com and create an author page and link it to your book. This will give your readers more information about you, your books, events, blogs, etc.

15. Order proofs in print to make sure it is set up exactly as you desire. Get ready to promote.

Chapter Three
Asking for Reviews

I've had many authors tell me that they have lots of friends who have promised to leave a good review for them. Some have even told me they could get 200 reviews. That has never happened in my experience. People readily say they will provide reviews, but when it comes to doing it, only a few actually follow through. However, the more reviews you have the more people will want to buy your book. Rumors are that if you have around 25 - 50 reviews, Amazon is more proactive in pushing your book.

Amazon has been very strict about what reviews they allow to be posted. They try to keep "friends" from leaving glowing reviews (even if they are true) and no one truly seems to know what their algorithm is for figuring out who is a friend or is not. Many reviews get taken down and if you protest, they usually reply that the reviews don't meet their requirements with no real explanation. It can be very frustrating.

I've read that Amazon looks at the time and date stamp on the link when someone writes a review. This means that if you copy the link (to your book on Amazon) and send the same link to twenty people, and those people use it so access your book, Amazon will see that they all have the same time and date stamp and may disallow them, assuming them to all be friends. I can't say for sure that this is true or not, but they certainly have very sophisticated software to find out who is connected.

A good way to make sure a review sticks is to have someone buy the book (although this is NOT supposed to be a requirement for leaving a review). Then Amazon will stick a "verified purchase" sticker on the review and it may have more weight with a reader. Here are the instructions to leave a book review. For your technically challenged friends, you may want to send them these instructions:

- Go to Amazon.com and log into your own account. You don't need to purchase the book on Amazon to post a review, however, if you do purchase through Amazon, they will add the lines, "Amazon verified purchase" to the review. Amazon reserves the right to take down a review if it is obviously done by a close friend/relative or from the same computer IP address.

- Choose the book you want to review and go to the book's page on Amazon.

- Click on the link next to the "stars" that says, "customer reviews" (just underneath the title and author). This takes you to another page with a button that says, "Create Your Own Review". Click the button.

- Click the number of stars you rate the book (five is the best).

- Create the title for your review.

- Fill in the box with your review.

- Click submit. You're done.

- You can also write a review without using your real name. In the upper right hand corner is a box to fill in a pen name.

Getting Professional Reviews

Yes, you can pay people to review your book, and if it is a good review, it may have some weight with a reader. Since we are talking about DIY promotions, however, paying $300-$500 for a review that may not turn out so positive, is probably not cost effective.

A better way is to search online for reviewers that are willing to read your book. Since many of these people and sites can get outdated quickly, I recommend that you search online for "free book reviewers." You can also look at Amazon's top reviewers but you'll have to do some digging because the list includes those that review all sorts of products, not just books. (http://www.amazon.com/review/top-reviewers). You'll have to click on the reviewer's name, go to their profile and see what they review and *IF* they have a contact email address.

A few sites that may review your book:

https://www.thekindlebookreview.net/book-reviews/

http://www.uncustomarybookreview.com/book-submission/

http://www.theindiebookshelf.com/p/submit-for-review.html

Some things to keep in mind:

1. Many reviewers do it because they love a certain genre. Make sure your book fits into what they want to read.

2. Follow their guidelines. Many want you to query them first with a book summary and author bio, a thumbnail of the cover and how many pages are in the book. Answer all their questions.

3. Keep a record of your queries so you know whom you sent one to and won't look like an idiot if they reply with questions and you don't remember them.

4. Don't bug them, especially if they are doing it for free. Many have others in the pipeline to read.

Have different formats ready for the specific way a reviewer wants to read it. They may request a PDF, a Kindle file (MOBI) or a print version. If you need to download a MOBI file, you can get one off your KDP (Kindle Direct Publishing) account. Under the "Previewer" section on your KDP account, you have the option to download the file as a MOBI file, which can be emailed to a reviewer.

Keeping track of your review requests:

Date Contacted	Contact Name	URL or Email	Action Taken	Follow Up

Date Contacted	Contact Name	URL or Email	Action Taken	Follow Up

To avoid having to write so much in each box of the chart, consider using codes or abbreviations:

Suggested Codes for Action Chart

Intro = Introduced myself

Ask= Asked whether I could guest blog for them

CB =Check back : Favorable response from blogger, send another email or contact later

SS= Sent sample of my writing

Chapter Four
Sending Out Press Releases

It used to be that you had to have "credentials" to send out press releases, but not anymore. There are many sites that allow you to upload a press release; they are free and the reason they are free is that they may show ads. If someone is searching for a particular topic and it pulls up your press release, most searchers are so used to seeing ads that they will likely just ignore them and see if your information meets what they are looking for.

Some Top Sites:

PRLog.com – You'll need to open an account with them but it is easy to do, just follow the prompts. They allow you to customize your press release with a photo, link or even an embedded video. Releases have a maximum 500-word limit. This is a well respected site by journalists. If you want to upgrade, for around $30, they will remove the ads.

Free-press-release.com

PR.com

If you use a free site, then you will wait in a queue for distribution, so make sure you leave several days leeway to send it out. Paid sites will give you more attention but a single press release can cost $300.

Press Release Format:

Every press release is expected to follow a fairly straight-forward format:

Contact: Name
Phone: XXX-XXX-XXXX
Email Address

FOR IMMEDIATE RELEASE

Title/Heading (Make it catchy!)

Date
City and State

Summary bullet points (optional)

Paragraph 1 (Intrigue them to read more)

Paragraph 2 (Give some details)

Paragraph 3 (Wrap it up)

Call XXX-XXX-XXXX for more information. (All body text: up to 500 words)

About the author/organization (short sentence to tell them who you are)

If you're an author, then announcing the sale of your book is one way to approach this, but be sure to make your book sound exciting. Show what problem your book is solving, do something clever, or write the body of the text first and then let the headline be created. Read other press releases, ads, social media and see what hits you. You should be able to come up with something unique, after all, you *are* a writer!

Sample Press Release

Contact: Jane Doe
Phone: XXX-XXX-XXXX
JaneDoe@XXXXX.com

FOR IMMEDIATE RELEASE

Fifteen Thousand Greyhounds to be Released from Jail

December 1, 2018
Tampa, Florida

Summary:

- Florida voters outlaw Greyhound racing, November, 2018
- Thousands of dogs held in cages
- Mass exodus of dogs means a crisis for dog shelters

November's midterm elections brought the state of Florida to an overwhelmingly unanimous vote to ban Greyhound racing in 2020. The existing dogs, estimated to number close to 15,000, will be released and many organizations will be frantically trying to find homes for these animals.

Unfortunately, just releasing these racing dogs does not mean that they will immediately make good house pets. Although Greyhounds have the reputations of being "couch potatoes," that doesn't just happen without some training. The training is to teach them how to be, well... just dogs.

Having lived most of their lives in cages with muzzles on, and by running on a track being their only physical outlet, these dogs have not had loving care or even learned how to play with toys. Training by Greyhound "halfway houses," where the dog is conditioned to love and care is a necessary intermediate stop on finding their forever home.

Call XXX-XXX-XXXX for more information.

Jane Doe is a dog-training specialist who helps abused animals "re-condition" their behavior to become the best pet they can be.

Write your press release:

_____

_____

_____

_____

_____

_____

_____

_____

_____

_____

_____

_____

_____

_____

_____

_____

_____

Chapter Five
Submitting Your Book for Awards

This is one area where you may have to pay an entry fee to get your book entered into a book contest. Costs can vary. Most awards are yearly. For example, the Indie Book Awards charge an entry fee of $75 per the first category entered and $60 for each subsequent category (https://www.indiebookawards.com). Getting an award or even being a finalist can help people take you seriously when they are browsing through lots of books.

If you search "Book Festivals" you will find numbers of book festivals all over the country, which may or may not have awards. You will need to go to each individual site to find out if they do have contests and what they require. Deadlines are usually strict.

Here are some other award sites:

http://globalebookawards.com/

http://www.writersdigest.com/writers-digest-competitions/self-published-book-awards

https://publishers.forewordreviews.com/awards/

http://readerviews.com/literaryawards/

http://ibpabenjaminfranklinawards.com/

http://indiereader.com/authorservices/indiereader-discovery-awards/

Award Planner:

Award Name/Contact	Entry Fee	Deadline	What Submitted	Date Entered

Chapter Six
Your Website

Every author needs a website. It can be simple but you still have to have one in this day and age. The best way of naming your site is to use the author name that will be on your books. If it is not available for some reason (you have a common name) then use your name and either "author" or "books" after it.

Make sure whatever website builder you use, it is optimized for mobile browsing. There are many easy hosting sites that offer drag and drop website builders, but you may want to hire someone to help if you are not technically savvy.

Some of the basics you need:

- An "about me" page or section

- A way to collect email addresses (you may want to send out pre-publishing information for additional books in the future , keep in touch or promote your book)

- Information about your book(s) with clickable links to buy

- Blog page (offer an RSS feed so that people can receive new blogs by email)

- Icons for your social media accounts (links that will take the viewer directly there)

Website Builders (some are free for basic service, some charge a fee):
- Wix.com
- GoDaddy.com
- Web.com
- Squarespace.com

- Wordpress.org

The principles of Search Engine Optimization - SEO:

Search engines (i.e. Google, Bing, Chrome, etc.) find suggested content (results) for you when you input a word, phrase or sentence into a search bar. As an author, you want to come up in the searches in the first page of results, ideally, because a great majority of people stop there. I always search through several pages because history tells me there is much to be found deeper in the results, but that is not the norm.

To be able to come up as close to the top of the results as possible means you have to be smart about how you use keywords (which can be a word, a phrase or a sentence). You are a detective who needs to figure out the most likely way a person could search and find your website, blog, or book in the results of those searches. The more exposure you have, the more likely to sell your book.

In all cases, you need to create an extensive list of keywords. Try to create several hundred. At first, you will think this is a daunting task but let the tools do the work for you. For example, if you search using Google for "dog training," the search bar itself starts to suggest phrases for you, usually about ten of them. It will be phrases others have actually used to search for dog training or related topics. Search for your own keywords that you think people might use for your book. Copy all those to a Word document or spreadsheet (Excel).

Next, go to another type of search engine such as YouTube and search for the same words (phrase or sentence). Are there different keywords? Copy those down. You can also use tools such as Google Adwords or Keyword Finder (KWFinder.com) or Moz (Moz.com – you will have to set up a free account) and copy their lists.

Using my example, on KWFinder.com, the top fifteen phrases that come up when you search dog training:

1. Dog training

2. Puppy training

3. Dog training near me

4. Potty training puppy

5. Dog training classes

6. Dog obedience training

7. Therapy dog training

8. Dog obedience school

9. Puppy training classes

10. Potty training dogs

11. Pet Trainer

12. Dog behavior

13. German shepherd training

14. Dog school

15. Dog obedience classes

Now, keep adding to your list. You could search for other terms, which in my example might be "raising a well trained dog," "bad dogs," "correcting dog behavior," and on and on until you have as many keywords as you can accumulate. Using the different keyword finder tools actually did show some different results for dog training. One list ranked "dog training commands" and "dog training tips" very high and they did not show up on the other lists in the top fifteen results.

Now, go to Amazon and search in the book department for your keywords. You may get a different set of keywords there too. Copy those down.

Now look at the books that come up as bestsellers or highly ranked in your keywords. Copy down the author names and the book titles. *Those just became keywords too.* Also, look at the reviews of books similar to yours to see if there are any keywords, phrases or sentences that seem to recur.

Save this list. Make sure your website has a "keyword" feature or plug-in that can be added to your website template to input keywords. Use as many of these as you can here. You will also use this list if you use any type of advertising such as Amazon Marketing Services.

My Website Planner

Name of my website (Is the domain name available?) Check: https://www.domain.com or the site you will use to build it should have a search bar for domain names):

_____

_____

Websites that I like (consider designing yours in a similar manner):

_____

_____

_____

_____

_____

_____

About me (what makes you different, what do you want people to know about you):

_____

_____

_____

_____

_____

_____

_____

_____

_____

_____

_____

_____

Blog topic ideas:

_____

_____

_____

_____

_____

_____

_____

_____

_____

_____

_____

_____

_____

_____

_____

_____

_____

_____

_____

Social media accounts to include:

_____

_____

_____

Keywords:

Chapter Seven
Using Social Media

Using social media is a way to get maximum exposure with a little effort and nowadays people EXPECT an Internet presence. Most of the authors I work with don't enjoy doing the effort because of the learning curve, but once you figure out what you're doing you can use tools so that you don't have to spend all day tied to a digital device.

The benefit of social media is that you can get exponential exposure by someone sharing your post. For example, if someone has thousands of followers and they share or "retweet" your post, then you just reached all their followers as well as your own. That's what makes a post go viral and reach millions. Of course, a viral post has to be something that appeals to the masses and that often means it includes a human-interest story of perseverance, something with animals or kids, or a story that evokes emotion.

Using any social media involves being clever in how you present yourself. Look at other's social media pages and see what catches your eye. Your ability to make yourself stand out by being witty, funny or different may gain you more followers. People want to be educated or entertained on social media so keep this in mind with everything you write about yourself and when composing your posts.

Depending on the age of your audience, you may need to use a different type of social media than you are used to. **Here's the difference in the generations:**

- **Silent Generation – Born 1925- 1945**

Social Media used primarily for news, health information, travel arrangements

- **Baby Boomers – 1946- 1960**

Spend more time consuming content, may tweet more than any other generation, engage in longer conversations on social media

- **Generation X – 1961- 1981**

Largest Pinterest audience (females), 86% are online daily, social media use spikes between 8 pm and midnight, 65% use Facebook

- **Generation Y (Millennials) 1981- Mid 1990s to 2000**

Usage spikes between 8 pm- midnight, expects more social consciousness, brand perception is formed on social media, crunched for time (they will skim articles, 57% will watch video)

- **Generation Z (iGeneration) Mid 1990s or 2000 to mid 2020s**

More likely to view a video, least likely to read, Twitter use is falling, Facebook is considered old-fashioned, they are strong on Instagram and YouTube

To determine what kind of content you post on social media, figure out who your readers are:

What age group do they belong to? Are they local, national or international? Is what you post providing value to them? Where does it add value to their lives? Do they have any special interests? What kind of questions would they ask you if you were face to face? Do they have a special set of challenges or issues that your book solves? Try to actually create your ideal reader by age, demographics, interests, income and more. Then look at your posts and wonder if the ideal reader would want to see them.

Look for content (search online)– blogs, videos, articles, memes, quotes, inspirational messages, cartoons, etc. that YOU would want to see. Is it visually appealing? If you have to click through lots of pop ups when you click on an article/blog, it's likely not going to engage your followers.

Don't overly promote your book; people will get bored easily and unfollow you. You must add value to their day. Find fresh, relevant content. If an article you want to use has to do with technology and is more than a couple years old, it's probably not up to date any more. However, if an article deals with time tested and classic concepts, then it's probably okay. You can tell immediately when you click on a site, blog or article if it looks old fashioned or up to date. The "look" of a site will let you know approximately when the content was created. Beware of copyright infringement. Make sure to give credit to others by providing the original link.

What I often do to find content is to Google a topic and then skim over the first couple of pages of results to find something I might want to post. If I don't find something within the first thirty seconds or so, I move on to another topic. Since my posts have to do with subjects such as writing/publishing, small business, franchising, entrepreneurship, I search for different subjects first. Some of my searches might be: writing tools, writing ideas, how to write better, how to publish easily, or writing to make money. If I am searching for small business content, I might search for: small business ideas, small business trends, what's new in small business, things to look out for when starting a business. You get the idea, try to re-phrase things in several different ways until you find something interesting. Then click on the link and skim the article/blog/content, etc. to see if it really fits. This is not too time consuming once you get used to doing it and you are rewarded with engagement from your followers (if they like your content).

Look for authors in your genre that you can emulate (NOT steal their content, always give them credit). You might want to follow them on social media or subscribe to their blog so you understand what the marketplace offers and wants. See how much engagement they get from different posts. Always think about "educate or entertain."

Images are key:
Remember that "pictures are worth a thousand words" and make sure you use images in your posts that represent what you are trying to say, catch attention or make people want to read more. **Pixabay.com** is a great site of copyright free images that do not require attribution or licenses. Otherwise, make sure you give credit to the creator of the image or have permission to use it. Remember that many "stock" photos can be spotted easily and are not longer so interesting. People have grown accustomed to them and appreciate more natural images today.

Facebook:

Most people are familiar with Facebook. You should have a professional/business page, not just a personal page. The reason is that with a professional/business page, you can *schedule* your posts on Facebook as well as buy ads to show up on others' timelines. When you schedule your posts, you can create a whole slew of them and have them released when you want, over days or weeks. Do them all in one day and work several days ahead. You should also invite people to "like" your page.

You can also promote your book with even just a few dollars a day by creating an ad. Facebook must approve it before it is released as an ad and it can't have too much text. For anything you do, make sure you have a great image, GIF or video to catch people's attention. Your aim is to get people to interact with you, share your post or click on a link. You can create an ad based on demographics, interests, age, gender, etc. With Facebook's algorithms constantly changing about who will actually see your posts on the timelines of people who "like" your Author Page, ads are a good way to reach people who may never have heard of you, but might want to.

How to set up a Facebook professional/business page:

https://www.facebook.com/business/pages/set-up?ref=ens_rdr

How to create Facebook ads:

https://www.facebook.com/business/help/1361486070635113
(Be aware and always double check everything! Make sure when you put in the amount you want to spend, you are sure it says so much per day or how much in total you are willing to spend. If you are not careful, you can suddenly find yourself paying $900 when you meant to pay $90 in total).

Once you have set up your Facebook Author Page, you should post on that page for anything having to do with your book, being an author, writing, etc. This is open to the public so handle your posts accordingly. It is not wise to be controversial or political here. You want to sell books, not upset your readers. Have a goal to post at least 2-3 times a week.

Twitter:

I find it much easier to grow a following on Twitter. They do not have so many unusual regulations and it is easy to get thousands of followers if you do a little bit of work every day (approximately 15minutes). Authors and writers are very active on Twitter and very supportive. If you interact with other authors and promote their work on your timeline, they will often reciprocate. If you give good writing information, then others often retweet (share) it.

How to open an account:

https://help.twitter.com/en/create-twitter-account

How to find followers:

This strategy requires discipline but really works. Many people do not understand that you simply cannot wait for people to find you, you must be proactive. Go to the account of someone that posts about writing, an author with work similar to yours, or a resource for books. Find the account by searching for the name in the Twitter search bar in the upper right of your own account page. Click on that profile of the person you searched for.

You will see across the tool bar underneath their banner picture, that it says "Followers" and gives a number. Click on that. You will see all the people who are following that account. Scan the profiles of the people who are following that account, and if they seem "real" (have a profile picture and a real bio), click on "follow." You are now following these people/accounts. The reason you do this is because of reciprocity. The majority of Twitter users will follow you back and you will grow your own followers. I have grown to over 20,000 followers using this method.

Until you reach around 5000 accounts that you follow, Twitter will allow you to just keep "following." Once you reach that number, Twitter will want you to be in a ratio of approximate equivalency of those you follow and the those that follow you back. If you don't stay roughly the same, Twitter will prevent you from following too many more accounts without deleting some of your followers. When you reach this point, you need to "unfollow" those that you are following, but are NOT following you back, to keep the ratio correct. Go to ManageFlitter.com in another browser window. While you still have Twitter open, allow Manage Flitter.com to access your Twitter account (you many have to set up an account first) and then "unfollow" the oldest accounts that are not following back. ManageFlitter.com will show you who they are and allow you to just click "unfollow." They allow 25 "unfollows" per day for a free account.

Repeat this exercise daily and you will grow your followers rapidly. I also post content, retweet (share another's post) or tweet out a "thanks for the retweet" post. I make it a goal to tweet 4 times a day. The more you post (without being annoying), the more likely someone is to see your posts since people who follow a lot of other accounts have a big timeline to read!

Using Hashtags (not optional!):
In each post, you should use 1-4 hashtags. Hashtags are NOT something you make up. Never make up a hashtag unless you are being funny or entertaining. The whole reason for a hashtag is that it is simply a keyword or search term that is popular enough that people put them in a search bar to find information on that subject. When you put a hashtag in your post, people who are searching for that particular subject or hashtag, might be able to pull up your post, thus reaching you even though they didn't know you existed. Simply put the pound sign before a word to make a hashtag, NO SPACES even if it is several words together.

Popular Hashtags for Writers/Authors:
#AmWriting
#AmEditing
#ShortStory
#WritersLife

#WritingTip

#IndieAuthor

#AmReading

#FreeReads

#BookGiveaway

#YA

 #Crime

#LitFic

#AmReading

#WritingCommunity

#Writing

#Author

#AuthorConfession

#Writers

#WhatToRead

#ChickLit

#Suspense

#KindleBargains

#WomensFiction

#Books

#FreeBooks

#EBooks

#IndieAuthors

#Romance

#SciFi

#Horror

#History

#BookGiveaway

#WeekendReads

Also, try to tie your posts in with trends and use hashtags of the trending topic.

Make sure to check your Notifications and Messages daily, if possible, and respond to anyone that wants more information or is looking to connect with you. Someone just may want to interview you! Also, follow back people who followed you first, as long as they look like a legitimate person or account.

One Twitter site you should check out is AskDavid.com. This site will let you set up 30 tweets, which go out to their 58,000 Twitter followers, for a $10 fee. You can't beat that deal. They will also tweet about your eBook (for free) on those days when you offer it at no charge on Kindle Select.

Managing your social media calendar:

So now that you've got an account opened and you're supposed to make yourself visible by posting several times a day, you might be ready to pull your hair out. No one wants to be forced to check the computer at all hours of the day or be tied to their mobile device more than they already are. The best solution is to use a scheduling program. I use the paid version of Social Pilot (SocialPilot.co –*not* .com) and find it very easy to use. You can have multiple accounts (think pen names, causes, your business, etc. if you want to have more than one account) and then schedule posts to go out weeks ahead. At one point I scheduled posts for ten different accounts for an entire month and everything worked fine.

Another wonderful feature of Social Pilot is that it stores the posts that have been "posted" for several months so on any given day, if you just have nothing new to say, you can go back and "re-post" some of the older ones. If it's been several months, no one will know the difference. It speeds up posting time tremendously. Social Pilot charges $100/year.

Other scheduling programs are:

Buffer.com (there is a free version but you can't schedule as many posts ahead of time, but it also has a great feature called Pablo to help you create images with text).

HootSuite.com is another, but charges start at $29/month.

Pinterest:

Pinterest is a site that requires you to virtually create bulletin boards and then "pin" virtual content to a board. The boards are separated into different topics. As an author, if you choose to go this route, you will require a business account, a link to your website and the commitment to do LOTS of pins. For your pins to show up to someone searching on a subject, Pinterest wants you to do 10 pins a day, although they can be scheduled on a service so you could actually do 70 in one day with the scheduler.

I find this to be an almost overwhelming task and also see that most authors that use it find that their pins on food, cooking, crafts, etc. is what drives the traffic, not necessarily someone searching for a book to read.

How to set up an account on Pinterest:

https://help.pinterest.com/en/business/article/get-a-business-profile

Instagram:

Instagram appeals to a younger audience but it requires lots and lots of images. You will need more picture and videos to get attention and must find a theme or a central focus to pull followers to you. Can you commit to posting 1-2 times a day? You also have to use real time images, not stock photos because younger people have become almost immune to them. You can almost spot them a mile away. If you have an active life and can show all sorts of interesting things and activities, then this may work for you.

Make sure you set up a business page. Add the links to your book and website. If you feel up to this, add an email address where people can interact with you. If you value your privacy more, than forego that. Don't over promote your book; you have to find a clever way to be an "interesting" person, not just an author salesperson.

Hashtags rule here. Every post is jammed with hashtags, maybe 30 or more.

How to open an Instagram account:

https://help.instagram.com/155940534568753

LinkedIn:

Since LinkedIn connects professionals to other professionals, think of some of the ways it might benefit you. As you add to your network (you need to send an invitation to connect), you may find connections that can get you speaking engagements, help with services you need such as editing, other authors that can offer "been there, done that" advice, and many other types of things you may not have thought of yet. LinkedIn has a lot of credibility with the people on the network because you can see a person's profile (and resume) and you get to decide whether to connect or not.

An author can use this platform in a similar way to Facebook, but the actual connections to other professionals may be more solid. You can still post content on LinkedIn, and people can see your profile, which should heavily play up your writing/authorship skills. Some believe that LinkedIn profiles are weighted well on Google when it comes to people searching for you, so you should definitely have a LinkedIn profile (i.e. LinkedIn ranks well on Google).

How to set up a LinkedIn profile:

https://www.linkedin.com/help/linkedin/topics/6042/6043/15493/your-linkedin-profile-overview?lang=en

Planning Social Media:

What authors am I similar to (ones with blogs or good social media content):

_____

_____

_____

_____

_____

Websites I like for finding good content:

_____

_____

_____

_____

_____

_____

_____

_____

_____

_____

My list of hashtags:

_____

_____

_____

_____

_____

_____

_____

_____

_____

_____

_____

_____

_____

_____

_____

_____

Chapter Eight
Giveaways

Giving away a book may seem counterintuitive to some. I've heard some authors say they would never do it. They wrote it, they want to be paid for their effort. However, you have to get people talking about your book to have "word of mouth" advertising and lots of people monitor free book giveaway sites or look at Kindle Daily Deals on Amazon. Free books encourage people to download your book.

If you are writing a nonfiction book to show your credibility in a certain subject, then you especially want to give your book away to establish that foundation. You want to be known as the "expert" in a subject area. Having a book to wave around when doing a speaking engagement also shows you are serious about your subject, have taken the time to actually write an entire book, and helps people respect your work ethic.

Giveaways are also a way to collect and establish an email list. If you give your book away in exchange for an email, then you can keep in touch with the reader, especially if you plan to publish more books. A reader who enjoys your books, is a much easier sell than a brand new reader who is not familiar with your style.

The KDP Select program on Amazon allows you to either discount your book ($.99 is recommended) or give it away for free. You agree that Amazon will have your eBook exclusively for 90 days and your free or discounted promotion will run for five days out of the 90. You get to pick the days you want it to be free or discounted. Then you should promote it on book sites that have large email lists or on sites such as AskDavid.com, which will tweet about it for no charge on the days that it is free.

To find out more about using KDP Select:

https://kdp.amazon.com/en_US/help/topic/G201298240

You will want to promote your book with websites and bloggers that have large email lists of people looking for free or discounted books. Unfortunately, lots of these sites have not been updated and look pretty old fashioned. I tend to avoid those. But if you search online for "book promotion sites" you will find lists (I suggest adding the year at the end of that search term because sites change frequently). Look for how many names are on their email list. Is it worth what they charge? For example, RiffleBooks.com charges $150 to promote your free/discounted book but they say they have 500,000 on their mailing list. That's not even one cent per name. (https://www.rifflebooks.com/advertise

Other sites are:

Bargain Booksy: https://www.bargainbooksy.com/sell-more-books/ (Starts at $25, almost 300,000 on mailing list)

eReader News Today: https://ereadernewstoday.com/bargain-and-free-book-submissions/#toggle-id-3 (Starts at $40, mailing list of 200,000)

Free Booksy: https://www.freebooksy.com/for-the-authors/ (Starts at $30 for lesser known book categories, mailing list of 400,000)

Good Kindles: https://www.goodkindles.net (Advertising plans starting at $9.95 a month, their site states they have thousands of followers, your book does not have to be free to advertise here)

Most of these sites charge different amounts for the different categories of books, so a romance author may pay more than a horror author. They also charge differently based on whether your book is free or just discounted.

Many authors find it daunting to manage the technical side of things if they want to giveaway books. You must find a way that will allow the reader receiving the book to get it in the format they need. Many of those on the receiving end will have technical problems with a download but there are services out there that can streamline the process for you. BookFunnel.com is one of them. To find out more about them go to: https://bookfunnel.com/features/. They charge a fee but it is very reasonable, as low as $20/year.

Another site that gives away freebies:

Prolific Works: https://www.prolificworks.com/

Chapter Nine
Help a Reporter

One site that I really love is HelpaReporter.com or HARO (Help A Reporter Out).

Help a Reporter Out is a site that will give you daily emails (once you sign up) that are lists of topics that reporters/writers/producers are looking for, to get help on their projects. They say on their site that they "distribute more than 50,000 journalist queries... each year." They also say they reach "more than 800,000 sources and 55,000 journalists and bloggers" which makes their reach huge. Once you start receiving their emails each day or twice a day, you will see a list of queries that reporters are trying to get information on, or talk to "experts" about. You have the option of replying to them and if they feel you are a good fit, they will publish a quote, opinion, or comment from you and you will get lots of exposure.

Requests are categorized by topics:

The requests are separated by such topics as Biotech and Healthcare, Business and Finance, Education, Entertainment and Media, General, High Tech, Lifestyle and Fitness, Public Policy and Government and Travel. On any given day there may be more than one email sent to you and tons of requests. Read the paragraph that gives the reporter's pitch, see if you qualify as someone they want to hear from and then follow their guidelines. Most have deadlines, some are very fast and others give you several days to respond. You may know who the requesters are but some you do not. But you could get some free publicity and if your content is used, you will always get credit. It's good to show up like that in Google searches.

When I'm diligent about monitoring the emails, I often find ones that I can answer. When I reply, I get mentioned as an "expert" about two thirds of the time. It doesn't usually require much effort since often they only want a few sentences.

Here is a sample query from HARO:

5 Ways to Include Your Pet in Holiday Festivities (Parents.com)

When you click on the link in the email, it will then give you additional information on their requirements. Some will ask for a short bio, some will want your social media info, some will want to contact you.

Check them out:

https://www.helpareporter.com/

HARO Record Keeper:

Subject/Query	Date	Who Responded To	Deadline	Follow-up

Chapter Ten
Blogging

The whole point about blogging is to write about something the reader really wants to know about, NOT what you *think* they want to know. How do you do that? Use tools online that let you find out what people are searching for and then work it into your content to match the search.

How can blogging help?

For example, an author of detective novels says he used a well-known public figure to compare to the hero of his book, in his blogs. Fast forward to a huge scandal involving the well-known public figure and millions of people were searching on the Internet with the author's blog showing up. The author says he sold a *lot* of books just by being in the right place at the right time.

Make sure your blog is attached to your website, don't use a separate blogging site. The goal is to drive traffic to your information and *your* books, not some huge site with thousands of blogs.

You can use Google Trends to find out what is going on in online searches. Of course, a lot of those searches involve celebrities or music so make sure you find a topic that really can be connected to your book, your life, topics about writing, being an author, etc. People see through someone who just wants to capitalize on a famous name.

When you open Google Trends, scroll down till you come to the section "recently trending." You can keep scrolling backwards through the days to see what people are searching for. Since it was near Thanksgiving while I was looking at Google Trends, there were a lot of searches about Black Friday and turkey. Keeping with our theme of "dog training" that we used early on in this book, how would you create a blog about these trends with dog training in mind? You could write about what dog training aids are on sale on Black Friday. You could compose a blog about whether or not you should feed turkey to a dog. However, since those searches are calendar dependent you would have to release your blog immediately because the window of opportunity will expire.

You will find a difference of opinion on just how long a blog should be. Some say it should be 1000 words to get Google to increase your ranking on search engines. Others say it should be just 2-3 paragraphs and an image. I agree with the latter point of view. Plus, use the most eye-catching image you can find.

You can also use Google Adwords to find out how many people are searching for certain terms. You will have to set up an Adwords account to use it but don't set up a campaign, just use the tool. Go to "Find New Keywords" and input a topic. It will pull up how many people searched for the term as well as anything close to it. For "dog training" it shows "average monthly searches" of 10,000 - 100,000. It also ranks whether the competition is low medium or high, meaning how many others already have content using those words on the Internet. Ideally, a highly searched word or phrase with low competition is a good starting place.

What's really great is that the related terms that are searched for will give me ideas for my blogs that I may not have thought about. "Dog training" was followed by:
- puppy training
- dog training near me
- potty training puppy dog training classes
- dog obedience training
- therapy dog training
- dog obedience school
- puppy training classes
- potty training dogs
- pet trainer
- dog behavior
- German shepherd training

- dog school

The top seven terms all brought in searches of the same size audience as dog training and all had medium competition.

For Google to notice your blog, you must use the best SEO practices, making sure that if someone searches for dog training, then it recognizes that you are responding to that topic in your blog. Use it in your headline and then use synonyms or other closely worded phrases in the first sentence, the first paragraph and a few other times in your blog, so around 4-5 times. But DO NOT "keyword stuff" or use the keyword when it doesn't make sense or overdo it so that Google actually penalizes you instead of rewarding you.

For example, I could say in the title: Dog Training When You Just Don't Have Time. Then to rephrase it, I might say in the first sentence: Training your dog can be a hardship when you have to work twelve hours a day. However, a well-trained dog can really make your life easier. Google will recognize the same meanings.

So if you're not used to writing 300-500 words about topics, how do you think of an idea? You can use the bubble method I suggested early on or you, as a writer, can compose some blogs that appeal to a writer or reader:

For example:
- How I Came Up With My Book Idea
- How I Kept Writing with Kids in the House
- How I Created an Outline for my Book
- I Want to Write Like _____ So I Sold My Soul
- How to Write a Romance in Two Weeks

All these topics correspond to something you might have actually gone through and can write about credibly. Lots of other writers as well as readers, might want to know the actual creativity process, the system you use to write, the time of day you are most productive, if you have any rituals to start the writing flow, if you use any special lighting, décor or tools, etc.

Others might want to know how your travels influenced your book's locale, how food enters into what the characters eat, how your ancestry might affect the way your characters behave, etc. There are endless topics out there that you can always compose a few paragraphs about. You just need to do it.

Since Google rewards (in search engine rankings) more fresh content, the more you can blog (on your website) the more you have the opportunity to drive traffic to your site. The more traffic you drive, the more someone will see your book and the more possibilities for sales.

Go to Google Trends:
https://trends.google.com/trends/

Go to Keyword Planner:
https://ads.google.com/aw/keywordplanner/ideas/new?

You can also explore guest blogging – asking another blogger if they would consider posting a blog you wrote on their site. This will increase your exposure but it has to be something the other blogger likely doesn't write about. To find bloggers, just Google the subject followed by the word "bloggers." For dog training, I would Google "dog training bloggers." Then go to their site and find their contact form. First query them if they would accept a guest blog, then if/when they reply, pitch your blog in a short email. Some may want to see the whole blog before they commit to using it.

Remember, everyone is inundated with data, emails and information. Don't give up right away if you don't get a response but try again (and again).

Planner, blogs to write:

Topic/ Theme	Significant Points	Title of Blog	Keywords

Guest Blog Request Planner

Blogger/Contact	What Suggested to Them	How/When Contacted	Response	Follow-up

* Some of the most searched for blogs on the Internet include fashion, food, travel, beauty, music, fitness, lifestyle, mommy blogs, sewing and wedding blogs. The first three have the most searches, by a large margin. If you can relate your topic in some way to those types of blogs, you can reach a larger audience.

Chapter Eleven
Author Communities

Goodreads is touted as the largest community for readers and authors with twenty million members. As an author, your goal is to get people engaged and talking about *your* book. **You can set up an author page:**

https://www.goodreads.com/author/program

Your author page can show such content as where you were born, your book website URL, a profile picture (be careful about those awful pictures, get a good one!), your social media handles, the genres you write in and a bio. You can even connect your blog here!

You may do book giveaways, advertise your book for free, and host author discussions. Goodreads also has a section called Listopia, where the books are ranked in each genre by reader votes. You can get your book on the lists.

BookBub is a book recommendation site. I use it as a reader and get daily recommendations as to one discounted book daily, many of which I end up buying. There is a section for authors to give updates about their books, what they are working on and any other information. You can advertise your book here, but the cost can be pretty steep.

You can sign up for an account:

https://partners.bookbub.com/users/sign_up

Bublish offers a free "emerging author" account or for $99/year you can get a full-featured author account. They have a book promotion section called "book bubbles," (show an excerpt, talk about your inspiration, give a book summary, etc.), you can post an author profile, and track reader engagement with analytics. What I really enjoy about Bublish is the information they give you for free. There are webinars and blogs, all with very pertinent information.

Get an account:

https://www.bublish.com/

Facebook Author Groups can create some opportunities for cross promotion with other authors. In Facebook, use the search bar to input "author groups" and go down the list and check them out. You will also find all sorts of questions and answers from other authors. Most all of the groups say to refrain from posting religious or political content. Some are very strict about not posting your own book. All of them say they can boot you from the group if you don't adhere to their policies.

Some Facebook Writing/Author Groups:

Writers Helping Writers – closed group, must agree with policies to join (no self promotion).

Writer's Group –must agree with policies, closed group.

Authors – public group, must still adhere to their policies.

Indie Author Group – closed group, same as the rest.

Author Community:

Author Site	Login/Password	Author Profile Complete?	Things to Do

Chapter Twelve
YouTube

Although a lot of people consider YouTube to be part of social media, I think it deserves a chapter by itself. YouTube is becoming a great search engine and with the popularity of watching videos, it is a great platform to get exposure. However, because there is so much competition out there, you must have a "hook" or reason for people to watch YOU. You also need to have a Google account (Gmail) to be able to set up your own channel.

First of all, be professional. If you are going to make videos, make sure you have some basic equipment so people will watch and not turn you off. Get a tripod and use it religiously. You can get mini ones for your phone or ones that have flexible legs to wrap around poles or tree branches or even tripods to put on your car's dashboard. If you use a regular video camera, then invest in a tripod that can be adjusted easily on uneven ground.

If you use the camera on your computer, check out the back view of your room and look at what the viewer sees. Lots of junk lying around behind you? Are you in your bedroom with your unmade bed showing? Nothing loses credibility like showing someone how poorly you decorated your home or that you own practically nothing. Set up a staged backdrop or buy a backdrop that you can hang behind you.

You must have adequate lighting. If you don't have it from a window or powerful enough lamps/overhead lights, then get some studio lighting. It's not all that expensive and most lights now come as LEDs and save energy and do not get too hot. Three point lighting means there is a backlight behind you (low and pointing upwards), one off to the left side in front of you and another off to the right side in front of you, as though they were in a triangle, with the camera set to record you from a front facing position.

Sound quality must be good. You can't have interference, buzzing noises or be so soft spoken that people can't hear what you are saying. Make sure you have good acoustics, not a lot of echo and use something to absorb sound (such as carpet or blankets). If you live in an area with lots of noise, look into using a setup that uses a microphone surrounded by sound dampening foam (foam that looks like egg crates). Some people throw a blanket over their head with the microphone to cancel out external sound. Some audio recording programs such as Audacity.com have noise canceling functions.

You can create short videos (two minutes is ideal) about the same topics that you would normally blog about. Instead of writing, you're just talking. Keep practicing and keep recording until you sound relaxed and can pace your voice at a normal speed. Make sure you are dressed appropriately (the same way you would for a casual business meeting) and do the same things, grooming wise, you would do if you were having your picture taken. No one wants to see you at your worst.

Some authors do book reviews of other author's books as a means to pop up in an online search of a famous author/writer. You can do a quick two-minute review or have some type of theme for your YouTube channel. For example, you might act out some of the characters of a bestseller, or do a reading from the book or change a character's role to be humorous. You may have seen some of the stars of YouTube acting out a commercial in a funny, silly way or people who attempt to do a stunt, even though they have no ability. Do something to capture people's attention.

Some equipment to check out (you don't have to have any of this but it could make your video life easier):

1. Rode SmartLav+ Lavalier Condenser Microphone for Smartphones Tablets - Omni-Directional (allows you to step farther away from your Smartphone)

2. Blue Yeti USB Microphone (for your desktop/laptop). Your integrated microphone is just not the best quality.

3. Audio Technica Lavalier Microphone- ATR3350 (low cost with approximately 15 feet of wire that I use with my Canon video camera). Uses a battery which needs to be turned off after each use or it will run down completely. Very good sound quality for the cost!

4. SmartPhone Tripod, UBeesize Portable and Adjustable Camera Stand Holder with Wireless Remote

5. JOBY GorillaPod SLR Zoom Flexible Tripod for DSLR (regular cameras that take video)

6. Photography Photo Portrait Studio 600W Day Light Umbrella Continuous Lighting Kit by LimoStudio

7. Julius Studio Photo Video Studio 10 ft. Wide Cross Bar 7.4 ft. Tall Background Stand Backdrop Support System Kit with Carry Bag (backdrop setup w/o backdrop)

8. Julius Studio 6 x 9 ft. Photo Studio Chromakey Background Muslin Backdrop Bundle Kit, Black, White, Green, Gray (I love using a green screen so that I can delete the background and use my own, then I can be anywhere!)

9. Camtasia video editing software - https://www.techsmith.com

YouTube Planner:

Topic/ Theme	Significant Points	Title of Video	Keywords	How Long?

Chapter Thirteen
Public Speaking

Are you a nonfiction author? Are there industry associations that relate to the topic you write about? Then see if you can get on their agenda. You will likely have to check this out months and months ahead because conventions start to book as soon as the last year's event is completed. Are you willing to travel there? Are you willing to speak for free? Do you have a YouTube channel so they can see the way you speak and look? If not, you'll have to create your own media reel to send them.

You'll need to practice and practice your topic. I suggest you create several different length speeches so that you can correspond to whatever time slot you are given. Have a ten or fifteen-minute segment, a half hour segment and a 45-minute segment. Make sure you throw in some humor, some type of hook to keep them interested and make sure you give them some knowledge they wouldn't otherwise have. Consider joining a local Toastmasters group to get practice in front of real people.

Are you a member of the local Chamber of Commerce? You might approach them to see if you have a topic that would be pertinent to their members. You can approach networking groups, charitable organizations, and businesses to see if they have an avenue for you to speak at. If you can polish your speech to a professional level, you might get good referrals too. The more you can get testimonials, the more options you have.

Look for organizations within your city such as public relations professional groups, lunch and learns, networking groups, associations of coaches or consultants, conferences that are coming to town, leadership institutes, library lecture series, churches, non-profits, retirement homes, etc. There are endless opportunities if you are willing to put yourself out there.

One of the first speeches I gave about my first book (written about a true family scandal after World War II), was to a senior center. When I saw the advanced age of the audience I was worried, but it ended being an excellent venue to learn what questions came up and see their interest. They were also old enough to relate to the war (many being children or young adults during that timeframe) and got a lively discussion going.

Are you a fiction writer? Many give readings from their books mixed in with true-life stories of how a character was created, how you came up with the storylines, etc. You can approach book clubs, churches, organizations, and bookstores to get started and see what questions you receive; that may be a reason to expand your speech and branch out in new ways.

Directory of Trade and Professional Organizations (might find it in a library too)

https://www.associationexecs.com/national-trade-and-professional-associations-directory Cost $349

Online NonProfit Directory:

https://www.guidestar.org/NonprofitDirectory.aspx

FreeSpeakerBureau (find out who is looking for speakers)

http://freespeakerbureau.com/

Speaker Match (starting at $99/year)

https://www.speakermatch.com/

Podcasts are important. The fact that they can be listened to while doing another task makes them rising in popularity again. There are lots of part-time podcasters looking for their next guest, too. Most are an interview style format and you will likely receive all the questions ahead of time, making it less stressful than giving a speech. Many recordings will be edited before being broadcast, which again, makes it a more relaxed format. Most will be done over the phone or on a service such as Skype.

Look for a topic on Podcast sites such as iTunes, Spreaker or Sticher. You can also Google "podcasts." If you go to Spreaker.com, you can scroll through all sorts of categories to find relevant podcasts. Then click on the podcast icon to find out more.

If it looks like a good fit, then Google them separately and you will find a contact form to find out if they are looking for new guests. Start by a quick query to see if they are looking, and if so, could you pitch to them. If you get a yes, send an email with: your contact information, bio and credentials, links to your media sites or articles about you, your social media, and the subject you want to speak about. Then, don't bug them for a couple of weeks. If you don't hear back, you could send a short email saying, "Hey, I'm still interested."

Podcast sites:

https://spreaker.com

https://www.stitcher.com/

https://www.apple.com/itunes/podcasts/

It's also very easy to set up your own podcast on these sites. Then you can control who you interview and you always get to start or end with your bio that says you are an author and what your book is about. Or, you can start your own radio show at: http://www.blogtalkradio.com/. All this takes dedication and discipline to continue to find good content and faithfully upload you work.

Speaking Engagement Planner:

Query Sent To Whom?	Date	What For?	Follow-up Needed	Response

Chapter Fourteen
Author Central

Author Central is where you set up your author page on Amazon (https://authorcentral.amazon.com). You must have published your book first. You can post all sorts of information here: bio, photos, events, a blog feed, social media links, and links to all your books on Amazon.

The author page will show up near the bottom of the book page on Amazon. It will allow a reader to click on a link, which then takes them to your Author Page. What is positive about this, is if you write a series of books, they will all be listed here and the reader can instantly click on them to find out more or to buy them. Amazon will connect your book(s) for you.

If a reader loves your work, then an author page is essential to keeping them engaged. Let them know about what's coming soon or what you are up to. The more you connect, the more likely people are to feel they "know" you and support you.

Your bio (unique or relevant to your writing):

_____

_____

_____

_____

_____

_____

Pictures to upload:

_____

_____

_____

_____

_____

_____

Videos to upload:

_____

_____

_____

_____

_____

Social media links:

_____

_____

_____

_____

_____

Links to blogs:

_____

_____

_____

_____

_____

_____

Chapter Fifteen
Amazon Marketing Services (AMS)

If you're an avid reader like me, you'll note that a lot of book suggestions you receive from Amazon say "sponsored" on them. That means an author has paid money to put that suggestion (ad) there. You can also search for a specific genre or book and see sponsored books. Sponsored books show up beneath the "also bought" section and at the bottom of book searches (which are organic searches).

Basically, there are two main ways to advertise your book on Amazon, either by *"sponsoring"* or by a *display ad*. A display ad is just like placing an ad in any type of media. Display ads will show up near the "Buy" button of a specific book you want your ad to be next to (and also show up on Kindle screen savers). Advertising can be done so that it shows up in search results, related book detail pages, for people searching specific keywords, specific interests or specific books. Everything is done on a pay per click system (PPC) so you only pay when a reader actually clicks on your book ad.

Sponsored ads must have a list of keywords that you want your book to show up under, when those keywords are used in a search. It's interesting that they allow you to list other author names, books, or even publishing companies as part of your keyword list. If you go to the link I have included about Amazon advertising and scroll to the section that says "Resources," then click on the "Sponsored Products Link," you can download and print a short guide to choosing keywords and planning your strategy.

Amazon even allows for "negative" keywords now, which means keywords that you absolutely DON'T want your book ad to show up under. For example, if you are not giving your book away for free, you might use the term "free book" as a negative keyword. Now, think of any type of keywords that are "negative." That means that for any reason if someone searched using the negative keywords, you would NOT want your information to pop up. This is primarily so you don't pay for anything that won't benefit you. There may not be any, but you need to at least consider it. Another example, if you have a "clean" romance book, you may not want to pay for someone to click on it if they are looking for "erotic romance."

If you want to spend more ($100 minimum) then you can place a display ad and have it come up alongside a bestseller, if desired, or any other specific book. Hopefully your cover image and witty copywriting will convince someone to look at your book also, or buy your book instead. Click on the link below (about Amazon Advertising) and scroll down to "Ad Policies" and then click on "Go To Ads Policies." You're going to find quite a few restrictions. Ads are not allowed on several book categories or if you use any negative language (such as erotica, promoting drug use, hate speech, abusive manners, etc.)

You cannot advertise in categories such as diet and weight loss, personal misfortune such as bankruptcy, sexual dysfunction or dating and relationships. You cannot show certain images in your ad such as weapons. You cannot show provocative images. You'll find the complete list in Amazon's document.

If you want to use the AMS service, search for case studies on Google (Amazon Marketing Services, books, case studies) and see if you think it might be right for you. One case study said it would not provide any profit for you if your book is priced rather low and also mentioned that this author found success more for a series of books rather than a standalone book.

Finding the right keywords are important and Merchant Words for Amazon (see below) provides a service for about $30/month. Most authors need to use 300-400 keywords so consider finding a good source.

Find out more from Amazon:
https://advertising.amazon.com/lp/authors/

Merchant Words for Amazon Keywords:

https://www.merchantwords.com/

My Keywords for AMS:

Keyword	Keyword	Keyword	Keyword	Keyword

Keyword	Keyword	Keyword	Keyword	Keyword

Keyword	Keyword	Keyword	Keyword	Keyword

Keyword	Keyword	Keyword	Keyword	Keyword

Chapter Sixteen
Landing Pages

If you've researched marketing lately, you'll hear the term "landing page" quite frequently. Basically, a landing page is a one page sales technique that you "land" on when you click on an ad's link. If you have a Facebook timeline, you will see *sponsored* ads that show up there because of your browsing history. Facebook puts the ad on your timeline because it feels you are relevant to whatever the advertiser is trying to sell (or give away).

You'll often see ads phrased, "Free Just Pay Shipping," "Best Gadget Ever," "Five Thousand Already Sold," and every permutation there of. If it interests you and you click on the ad, or a "shop now" button, you will be taken to the landing page. You will usually have to input your email address before gaining access to the page especially if it is a free product. The advertiser will collect all those email addresses and then market more products to you or continue to show you how they can help you.

Why consider using a landing page?

What's critical about a landing page is this: it's a one-stop shopping page, you never have to click on anything else to be able to buy the product, get it for free, or take advantage of an offer such as a free PDF, free video, etc. The advertiser doesn't want to take the risk that you will see any other information that may distract you from taking the offer (they don't ever want you to click off of the landing page). The advertiser wants to make it as easy as possible to accept what they are offering.

So how can a landing page help an author? Especially if you are a nonfiction author with other products to sell (coaching services, consultations, other books, seminars, webinars, video courses, etc.), you can use the landing page technique to drive more sales (you will also hear the term "sales funnel").

You give them an offer that drives them to click on the ad. That takes them to the landing page where you have them sign up to receive the freebie or discounted product, THEN after they are intrigued by what you say, you give them the offer of your book (or maybe your book IS the freebie), then tell them what else you, as an expert, can do for them and promote your other products while they are a captive audience.

What you'll need:

- A page on your website that is not connected to the Home page (or use a service that provides landing pages)
- A freebie or offer that will entice people to go to the landing page
- A means to place an ad either on social media (Facebook, Instagram, Twitter) someone's blog or a way to send an offer to a substantial-size email list
- Depending on what your offer is providing, a way to either download the product, show them a video or cost effectively ship them what you offer
- A way to capture their email address (if you have a Wordpress website, there are multiple plug-ins to accomplish this)
- An email marketing program such as Mail Chimp, to send out newsletters, information, more offers, etc. to the email addresses that you accumulate. You must, by law, allow those you send emails to, to unsubscribe from your list. That is why you really need to use an email marketing program such as Mail Chimp which comes with that feature. Other programs such as Constant Contact charge a fee. Mail Chimp is free, up to 2000 subscribers.
- A way to "host" the product if it is a large-sized file, such as a video. (You can always host a video on Vimeo or YouTube, make it a private account, and then email the buyer a link to access it.)
- A way for the buyer to pay that is safe and carries an SSL certificate (multiple merchant service plug-ins are available on Wordpress or from the website host.)

Example: An ad to get people to your landing page. Using the dog training theme again, here is a sample. They copy should be something that emotionally engages them so that they don't hesitate to click on the button. The "click here" button takes them directly to the landing page. Your copy must be compelling enough to make people take the time to click and then you must deliver.

The next step after the person clicks on the button, is to take the person to an email gathering form on the landing page, usually a type of "pop-up" that asks for the first name and the email address. Once that is filled in, the free information is shown or a message comes up that the information (or link) will be sent to the respondents email address.

Example: Here is a sample of an email collection form (usually a website plug in) which will feed into an email address collection system such as Mail Chimp. It is advisable to post terms and conditions somewhere on the page that say that the recipient agrees to receive emails from you, which may be opted out of at any time.

After the form is filled out, the pop up disappears and they will either access the information they want or receive a link in their email inbox. It should also show at least one other product/book you have, that you charge money for. For example, you might say that keeping your dog from getting bored is essential to keeping them from chewing passports, carpet, chair legs and more. Then you show your book which details dog behavior and how to interpret the warning signs of boredom. The book has a description and a "buy now" button, which is connected to a merchant service account or PayPal.

Or perhaps you also coach dog owners on how to keep dogs from getting bored and allow them to sign up for a one hour coaching session. You can also use your book as the freebie and let them download a PDF format or send them an eBook to their email address, and sell your other services on the landing page. **Sample landing page:**

Here's your 5 free tips - why your dog might chew:

1. He's emotionally connected to you and can tell by your behavior that something's up. Keep reassuring him and keep his schedule as normal as possible.

2. He's bored! Make sure to exercise him to tucker him out so he is happier to lay around when alone.

3. He's curious. Make sure anything that is not safe for him is put away.

4. He likes the taste of whatever he is chewing. Spray it with a bitter spray.

5. You haven't shown him that it is off limits. Use a can filled with coins (sealed) to shake when he does something he shouldn't. Use it regularly until the behavior stops.

GET OUR NEW BOOK - CLICK TO BUY NOW!

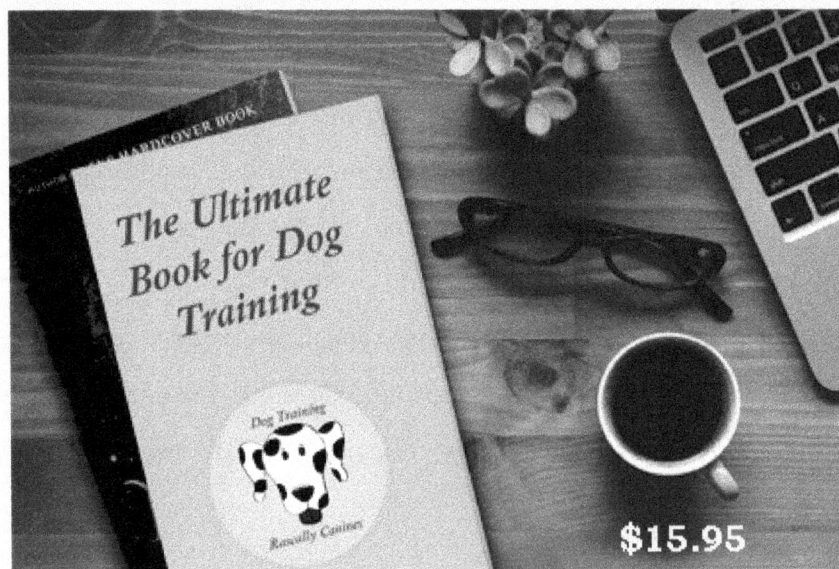

Find Mail Chimp here:

https://mailchimp.com/

Third party applications for creating landing pages:

https://www.leadpages.net (starts at $25/month)

https://landerapp.com (starts at $16/month)

https://www.launchrock.com/discover (free and this page also shows lots of examples of landing pages)

https://www.pagewiz.com/templates (starts at $30/monthly)

Create 3D mockups of your book for ads/landing pages:

https://covervault.com

What free or discounted offers can I give that are noteworthy?

_____

_____

_____

_____

_____

Copywriting ideas to get people to click on an ad (the hook or "why"):

_____

_____

_____

_____

_____

The other products I want to sell:

_____

_____

_____

_____

_____

_____

_____

_____

_____

_____

Where do I want to place ads?

_____

_____

_____

_____

_____

About the Author

Cynthia Readnower is an author, newspaper columnist, and owner of Skinny Leopard Media, a publishing company. She spent years in sales and marketing positions for Fortune 500 companies and received her M.B.A. from the University of Dayton.

Her first book encompassed her transition from seeing her family as "boring" to accepting that many secrets and scandals had been buried deeply in the family's past. Her second book was about her experience owning two franchised restaurants and what she learned (maybe more than she wanted to know).

As a publisher, she enjoys helping authors create their work and seeing the project from beginning to end; the glimmer of an idea, the work to get it down on paper, hammering out the details, the finished project and the magical look on an author's face as they hold their own book for the first time.

Follow her on Twitter: @CindyReadnower
www.CynthiaReadnower.com
www.SkinnyLeopardMedia.com

www.ingramcontent.com/pod-product-compliance
Lightning Source LLC
Chambersburg PA
CBHW051345290326
41933CB00042B/3230